Just Married

Just Married

A Sexy, Irreverent, Eye-Opening
Look at How We Met, Dated,
and Married the One We Love

Barry Sinrod
and Marlo Grey

Andrews McMeel
Publishing

Kansas City

www.andrewsmcmeel.com

98 99 00 01 / EBA 10 9 8 7 6 5 4 3 2 1

Library of Congress Cataloging-in-Publication Data

Sinrod, Barry.
 Just married : a sexy, irreverent, eye-opening look at how we met, dated, and married the one we love / Barry Sinrod and Marlo Grey.
  p. cm.
 ISBN 0-8362-5426-0 (pbk.)
  1. Marriage—United States. 2. Sex in marriage—United States. 3. Marriage customs and rites—United States. 4. Married people—United States—Attitudes. 5. Family life surveys—United States. 6. Sexual behavior surveys—United States.   I. Grey, Marlo.
II. Title
HQ536.S53 1998
306.81—dc21   97-38663
                                                              CIP

ATTENTION: SCHOOLS AND BUSINESSES
Andrews McMeel books are available at quantity discounts with bulk purchase for educational, business, or sales promotional use. For information, please write to: Special Sales Department, Andrews McMeel Publishing, 4520 Main Street, Kansas City, Missouri 64111.

Contents

Dedications and Acknowledgments

I dedicate this book to all my "oldlywed" friends in Boca Raton, Florida, and up north in New York. We still possess extremely sexy feelings, fond remembrances of when we were newlyweds, and most of us have newlywed children, and these two groups of people helped me develop the questions in this book. Married feelings do not change with age, as you will see. I have friends who married just a few months ago (for the second or third time) and lots who have been married 35, 40, 45, and even 50 years or more. All of us share the commonality of great love and support from our spouses, children, and grandchildren. My editor won't let me mention everyone who played a part in this book, but he will let me mention a few.

First and foremost I want to thank my new editor, Jake Morrissey, for his faith in me; a big thanks to the publisher, Andrews McMeel; and thanks to my agent, Christy Fletcher, of the Carol Mann Agency, who worked so diligently on my behalf.

Of course, I give extra special recognition to my life, my love, my bride of nearly 35 years, the sexiest of them all, my wife, Shelly.

To my wonderful children: Jodey, her husband, David, and their three children, Alex, Cole, and Jessie; my newlywed co-author daughter, Marlo, her husband, J.J., and the newest grandchildren, Chase and Landon; and my son, Blake, who is still single and playing the field at age 26.

My family is my total inspiration to write these wonderfully poignant and funny things. I love you all.

—Dad, Poppa, Barry Sinrod
(All the same person, different titles)

I dedicate this book to some of the most special people in my life. To my newlywed friends: Thanks for your input; I hope that you recognize your comments within our book (and that they don't get you in trouble!). To my sister, Jodey, brother-in-law, David, and their kids, Alex, Cole, and Jessie: Thanks for showing us the ropes and paving the way to married family life. To my brother, Blake: Although you are not ready for marriage yet, remember what Dad says: "The wife is always right"; with his advice you won't go wrong. Thanks also to my wonderful in-laws.

To my parents, who have shown me just how wonderful marriage can be between two people truly in love: The trust, compassion, friendship, and love you give to each other and to your children are an inspiration. I love you with all my heart.

And to my husband, J.J., who has made my life complete: As I say in this book, it was truly love at first sight, and I know I'll never look back. You are my *bescheirt,* my destiny.

And most of all to the sunshines of my life, Chase and Landon, I love you! You both mean the world to me! And no, you can't read this book until you are older.

—Marlo Grey

Introduction

Just Married began one evening when I was being driven crazy by preparations for my second daughter's wedding. It was more nerve-wracking than watching *Father of the Bride* because *I* was paying the bills. In addition, my wife, my older daughter (who has been married for nearly 10 years), and the new bride were all against me: I had no say when it came to selecting the catering facility, the band, the flowers, or the photographer. All I was allowed to contribute was the check to pay for it (with wonderful help from my daughter's future in-laws).

On this night the family was sitting around, and I was saying I needed to decide on the topic for my new book. I had several ideas, but one by one they rejected them all. Finally, my soon-to-be-married daughter asked, "Why not do a book about engagements and weddings?" The others chimed in with questions, suggestions, and ideas, and before long we had the outline of this book. I think the replies that came in to our survey questions are funny, poignant, crazy—and sexy.

The Facts

How did we find so many newlyweds? In this electronic age of data collection, you can find lists of just about anything. We pulled names of couples married less than two years from a variety of sources, including public court records, newspaper announcements, and magazines.

For this book we sent out 10,000 questionnaires to newlyweds of all ages, people who had been married from one day to two years. We got back 3,876 surveys—an almost 40 percent return—from all 50 states.

Our respondents sent back questionnaires via a pre-paid envelope (we paid postage), and they remained anonymous; we did not ask for their names. Thus, everything goes, no holds barred, because no names were required! We are confident they told us the truth. The statistical margin of error is plus or minus 3 percent.

Ready—Get Set—Go!

Now get ready for a wonderful ride, from the day a couple meets through the first years of their marriage. Whether your marriage is new or old, you will be able to see where you fit in today's world.

Remember to pick up a copy of this book when you go to a party or need a gift for someone in love, looking for love, ready to be engaged, engaged, planning to get married—or married for a short time, a long time, or forever.

Have fun!

P.S. If you have any questions or comments, please feel free to write to me, Barry Sinrod, at Department of Newlyweds, P.O. Box 811071, Boca Raton, Florida 33481. If you are on the Internet, write us at *sexwriter@prodigy.net*

1
In the Beginning

Courtship

How Did You and Your Spouse First Meet?

	Total
	PERCENT
Friends	25
School	15
Bar	10
Party	7
Blind Date	6
Other	37

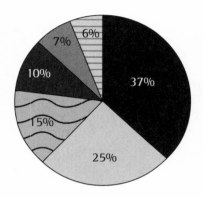

FRIENDS and OTHER are the most common ways to meet your spouse. I met my wife of nearly 35 years on a blind date, as did my newlywed daughter. But each category received its share of interesting answers. Here's a sampling.

We met at church when we were both four years old.

He was the foreman of the jury I served on. He asked for all our telephone numbers but only called me.

He was a lifeguard and I loved him at first sight: his pecs and his buns!

We shared a joint at a punk rock show.

He was my boss. He seduced me one night while we were working late.

We were in a bereavement group.

He saw me getting out of my RX-7. I was wearing skintight pants, and he said it was love at first sight.

Our teenage sons, who are good friends, fixed us up.

He fell on me at the mall.

We found each another through a video dating service.

We met at someone else's wedding.

We met during a march for women's rights in Washington.

I saw him on *The Oprah Winfrey Show* and called the station immediately.

I saw her at the food market and then at a drugstore within one hour and asked her out.

I followed her home from work because I thought she was absolutely gorgeous.

My roommate picked him up at the bus stop.

We were both coming out of the bathrooms at an Ohio Turnpike rest stop, and I ran straight into him, knocking him to the floor.

I answered a personal ad.

We were in the same Dale Carnegie class.

We met at a baby shower.

We were walking our dogs.

I delivered a pizza to him.

He gave me golf lessons.

I put her water bed together.

At the bowling alley, he dropped a ball on his foot and needed first aid. I'm a nurse.

I saw a photo of him in a local newspaper. I researched, found him, and called for a date.

He caught a ball at a baseball game and spilled his beer all over me.

At college we were kidding around and he dropped me on my head. Feeling bad, he took me out to dinner.

And here's a personal story. My older daughter met her husband when they were only 14 and 17, respectively. Their grandparents lived next door to each other in Florida, and they met while the families were on vacation. They continued to date briefly, once our family returned home to New York, but lost touch because of their age difference. Nearly six years later, my daughter ran into his brother at a dance club and shortly thereafter she "re-met" her husband-to-be. It was love at second (more mature) sight; she was 20 and he 23 and they married two years later. They now have three of the most beautiful children in the world and soon will be celebrating their tenth wedding anniversary.

Did You Kiss and/or Sleep Together on the First Date?

	Total
	PERCENT
Kiss	83
Sleep Together	17

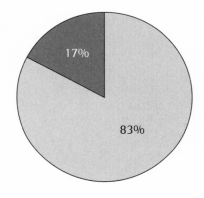

More men (88 percent vs. 82 percent) than women said they kissed good night after their first date, while more women (18 percent vs. 13 percent) said they ended the evening on an even friendlier note. This would mean that approximately 5 percent of the women slept with the man but he was not aware of it!

Older newlyweds (40+) and wealthier people (household incomes* over $75,000) were most likely to sleep together on their first date. Newlyweds who were married for the third time (or more) were also more likely to sleep together on the first date than those married for the first or second time.

*Throughout this book, "income" refers to household income.

How Long Did You Date Before Getting Engaged?

MONTHS	Total PERCENT
Less than 1	6
1–3	11
4–6	9
7–9	10
10–12	14
More Than 12	50

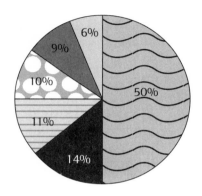

Half of our newlyweds waited over a year before getting engaged. What was the longest wait? Twenty-four years from the first time the pair met! This couple met at work when she was 19 and he was 44. He was already married, and she married about six years later. After they both divorced their spouses (he about 15 years after their first meeting, she about 22 years) they continued to be colleagues and friends until something "just happened." They finally became engaged when she was 44 and he was 69. At long last, they are happily married.

As to the rest of our respondents, several couples told us they skipped the engagement and married as soon as a few *hours* after their first meeting, and 91 percent of people over 40 got engaged within a year.

Fifty percent of those who have been married more than twice are quick to buy and/or get that ring; the man usually pops out the ring before six months are up. Those with the highest incomes, earning over $75,000 ($75K) annually, are the slowpokes (42 percent), dating an average of two years or more.

How Long Did You Date Before You Had Sex?

		Total
		PERCENT
	First Date	12
	1 Week	18
	1–3 Months	46
	4–6 Months	9
	7 Months or More	11
	Waited for Marriage	4

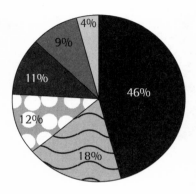

Women seem to be more aggressive about initiating love-making, according to the results of this question. Twice as many women as men (14 percent vs. 7 percent) said they slept together on the first date. *Most* couples, however, waited one to three months for the first time.

An interesting sidebar to this question: The older newlyweds (40+) were not only the most likely of the age groups to sleep together on the first date (20 percent) but also were the most likely to *wait* until the wedding night (11 percent). Go figure!

Wealthier people ($75K+) were the highest income group to do it on the first date. Virtually none of this income group (less than 1 percent) waited until marriage. At the other end of the spectrum, the lowest income group, making under $30,000 annually, were the least likely to make love on that first date.

Was It Love at First Sight?

	Total PERCENT	Men PERCENT	Women PERCENT
No	39	14	59
Yes	61	86	41

Well, *she* certainly makes a good impression!

Twice as many men as women claimed to fall in love at first sight. On a personal note, my newlywed daughter immediately knew when she first saw her spouse-to-be. She called her sister to report. "Don't tell Mom, but I'm going to marry him." Seven months later they were engaged.

My own wife recalled that when she answered the door to meet me for the first time, she told me to wait while she went back inside to get her jacket. Instead, she went and told her mother that I was going to be her husband. Well, it took me a while longer—30 days—to propose and another eight months to marry her. Now, almost 35 years later I love her much more than she could possibly know. You just can't predict when lightning will strike—and whether it will strike both of you at the same time. So the moral of the story is: Give love a chance!

Did He Ask Anyone for Permission to Marry You?

	Total
	PERCENT
Yes	28
No	72

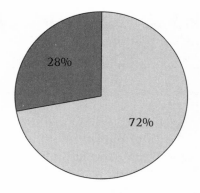

As would be expected, the highest number (37 percent) of those asking for permission to marry was among the younger newlyweds (18 to 24). Of those in the 40-and-older age group, 19 percent asked for permission to marry. And among those who have been married three or more times, not a single person asked for permission first.

My newlywed daughter recalls that her husband did not ask us for permission only because she told him that she wanted to be the one to tell us the news. Otherwise, he says, he would most definitely have asked.

As for me, nearly 35 years ago, I did not ask for permission. Perhaps it was because I had only known her for 30 days and was still in shock that I had actually proposed. When I think back to that time, I don't understand why her parents didn't object. I certainly would not give my daughters permission to marry someone they had known for only a month.

Did He or She Propose?
Did the Proposal Take Place on Bended Knee?

	Total
	PERCENT
He Proposed	92
She Proposed	8

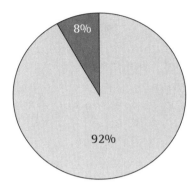

The 8 percent of women who did the courageous deed of proposing tended to be 40 or older, college educated, and married more than once.

Only a third (36 percent) of our male respondents proposed on bended knee. These "old-fashioned" proposers were the younger (18-to-24-year-old) set with medium-range incomes, college educations, and in their first marriage. And in case you are interested, one of the proposing women also did it on bended knee.

When You Were Asked,
Were You Ready to Accept?

	Total
	PERCENT
Yes	84
No	16

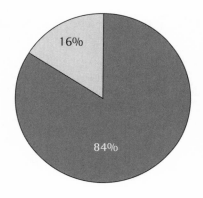

The element of surprise still exists for some newlyweds-to-be, but not for the majority. Although 16 percent of those proposed to were not sure if they were ready to accept, all of them (of course) ultimately did.

In just about all the cases, the couples who had already discussed marriage were ready, even if one was still surprised when the actual proposal took place.

Did You Get an Engagement Ring?
If Yes, How Big Was It and What Did It Cost?
Did He Take Out a Loan, Borrow Money,
or Go into Debt to Buy It?

Diamonds are still a girl's best friend. Eighty-four percent of our newlywed men presented an engagement ring to their partners. Those who didn't were older (40+) but not necessarily wiser. Of those who did buy a ring:

- 44 percent bought less than one karat
- 22 percent bought one karat
- 23 percent bought 2 karats
- 11 percent bought more than three karats

One person bought an eight-karat ring; one person needed help to carry her 12-karat ring!

The average cost of the engagement ring purchased by our hopeful grooms was $3,155.

Only 28 percent of the men had to go somewhere to get the money to buy the ring. And those who borrowed were older (40+) and richer (over $75K).

The Wedding

Who Got on Your Nerves Most in Planning the Wedding?

	Total*	Men	Women
	PERCENT	PERCENT	PERCENT
Future Spouse	14	18	12
Her Mother	32	50	25
His Mother	14	4	20
Other	41	33	45

*Adds to more than 100 percent due to multiple answers

I don't want to receive letters from feminists across the country, but the answers to this question clearly indicate that women create the most anxiety in planning the wedding. Just about every female possible contributes, especially *her* mother, *his* mother, and *her.*

The category OTHER manages to include a few men, but it is mostly chock-full of females. They include:

her best friend

her mother-in-law's friends

her mother's best friend

her other friends

her mom's friends

her mother-in-law's best friend

her other relatives—female, female, female, female

Did You Feel Any Pressure
As Your Wedding Day Came Closer?

Total (Both Men and Women)	
	PERCENT
No	44
Yes	56

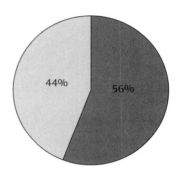

If Yes, Did You Ever Think of Calling It Off?

Total (Both Men and Women)	
	PERCENT
Yes	43
No	57

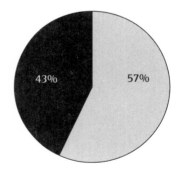

Nerves, nerves, nerves! Most of us feel them as the big day gets closer. Not only do the bride and groom suffer from nerves, it also seems that everyone associated with the wedding in any way, shape, or form is on edge.

A little more than half of our newlyweds (56 percent) felt the pressure, and among that group nearly half (43 percent) got cold feet. Slightly more females than males had second thoughts. But in the end everything worked out just fine.

Did You Have a Bachelor or Bachelorette Party?

	Total	Men	Women
	PERCENT	PERCENT	PERCENT
Yes	42	47	40
No	58	53	60

Nearly half of our newlyweds had a bachelor or bachelorette party. Only slightly more men than women had such a celebration, which surprises me, considering that you hear about bachelor parties (and what takes place at them) so often.

One of our male respondents had a bachelor party to which his father-in-law was invited. The party progressed, from bar to bar and house to house, and ended up at a mutual friend's place. Suddenly two female strippers came through the door and said hello, by name, to the father-in-law as soon as they spied him. It seems they had met on another occasion. I wonder where?

Did You Have a Traditional or Nontraditional Wedding?

	Total
	PERCENT
Traditional	54
Nontraditional	46

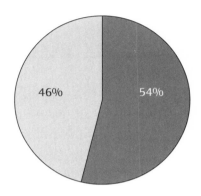

We were almost afraid to ask "What is traditional?" And when we did, we found out that nontraditional is surely in the eye of the beholder. Here's a sample of what our respondents defined as nontraditional:

We had to pay for it all.

We got married in one of those Las Vegas five-minute chapels.

We were married in a judge's chambers.

We didn't give each other rings.

We had our ceremony at Denny's restaurant.

We got married on my husband's farm, with the cows mooing.

We got married on the spur of the moment. Afterward we went to a motel, got drunk, woke up next morning, and called our parents.

My husband was in a total body cast on our wedding day. We couldn't have sex for two weeks.

How Many People Were at the Wedding?
What Did the Reception Cost?
The Wedding Dress?
Was the Garter Thrown?

- 8 percent of couples had no one else present
- 19 percent had fewer than 10 people
- 20 percent had between 1 and 50 people
- 22 percent had between 51 and 100 people
- 19 percent had between 101 and 200 people
- 12 percent had between 201 and 300 people

One wedding had 500 people in attendance; the average number of guests was 93.

When It Came to the Cost

- 10 percent said their wedding cost nothing
- 7 percent spent less than $100
- 23 percent spent between $101 and $1,000
- 30 percent spent between $1,001 and $5,000
- 11 percent spent between $5,001 and $10,000
- 15 percent spent between $10,001 and $30,000
- 4 percent spent between $30,001 and $50,000

One couple spent $75,000, and another couple spent $100,000; the average cost of the weddings for our newlyweds was $17,434.

As for the Dress

The wedding gown cost an average of $746, ranging from a hand-me-down cost of zero to a whopping $10,000.

And About the Garter

Garter removal is down substantially; only 41 percent participated in this old ritual. My older daughter did it at her wedding, but my newlywed daughter passed.

Did Anyone Try to Stop the Wedding?

	Total PERCENT	Men PERCENT	Women PERCENT
Yes	8	*	14
No	92	99	86

* Fewer than 1 percent of respondents

It appears that the men's relatives thought he had made the right decision with the right woman. But 14 percent of the women told us someone had actually tried to stop their wedding. We don't know who they were, but it didn't work.

Did Any Old Flames Attend the Wedding?

	Total
	PERCENT
No	79
Yes	21

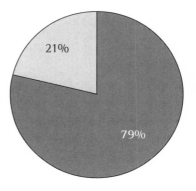

About one in five of our newlyweds remained friendly with former boyfriends and girlfriends and invited them to the festivities. Those most likely to ask old flames to their weddings were the youngest set, ages 18 to 24.

Did You Cry at Your Wedding?

	Total	Men	Women
	PERCENT	PERCENT	PERCENT
Yes	39	26	45
No	61	74	55

We cry at the movies and while watching television, why not at our own weddings? The most likely weepers are college-educated females, 25 to 34 years old, who are getting married for the first time.

At both *my* daughters' weddings, I cried like a baby. So did my wife, my other children, *and* the brides-to-be. Guess it runs in the family.

Who Paid Most of the Wedding Expenses?

	Total
	PERCENT
The Bride's Parents	33
The Groom's Parents	10
The Married Couple	57

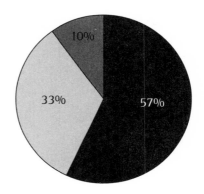

Having married off two daughters New York Jewish style, I only wish I could have been so lucky! Our national survey indicates that the marrying couples paid the major share of their wedding costs. Other interesting statistics from this question indicate that 22 percent of *her* parents paid for the entire wedding, as opposed to less than 1 percent of *his* parents.

One young new wife told us that dear old Dad had to finance five weddings in one year. She and her four sisters were all married within a 12-month period. Her dad is probably in the poorhouse. Five daughters married in one year?

For those marrying the second and third time around, it should be noted that parents on both sides left it to the marrying couple to foot the bill.

What Was the Cheapest Wedding Gift You Received?

We can't pinpoint who these cheapskates are, but here is a sample of what our respondents said they received as gifts:

nothing	salt and pepper shakers
a tacky sheet set	a $5 dinner bell
an empty picture frame	$20 from a best friend
a set of cheap glasses	$20 from the best man

One wife said, "We had 250 guests, and combined they gave us a grand total of $600! Give me a break—that's $2.50 per person, less than my invitations cost." According to another couple, "Everyone at our wedding was a cheapskate." And a third noted, "Our best man wanted us to pay for his tux."

What Is the Most Embarrassing Thing That Happened to You on Your Wedding Day?

We have all experienced an embarrassing moment when we simply wanted to hide in the closet and hope no one saw what happened. But can you imagine any of the following incidents occurring on *your* wedding day?

Well, for some of our newlyweds, they did. Here are a few tidbits from what they told us:

> The pastor walked in on me while I was getting dressed for the wedding. I was completely naked.

> My boobs fell out of my dress as we were taking family pictures.

> My husband stepped on my dress, pulling it off in slow motion. This made us both fall onto the floor in the church right before we were to walk back down the aisle.

> During his toast our best man announced that we were going to have a baby in a few months.

> During the ceremony my husband-to-be shouted at the top of his lungs that the ring burned and he had to take it off.

> At the beauty parlor, everyone in my bridal party was in a rush and very nervous. I went to the bathroom, and when I returned everyone had left. They forgot me: the bride. A customer in the store had to take me home.

> My dad's check bounced after the wedding reception.

> I forgot my bra and had to use masking tape to hold me up.

> My cousin asked me if I was pregnant in front of all my guests. I was not.

> I had an uncontrollable fit of laughter during the ceremony.

> My garter fell off as I walked down the aisle.

> He tried to put the ring on the wrong hand and panicked when it wouldn't fit.

The Honeymoon

Were Either of You a Virgin When You Got Married?

	Total
	PERCENT
No	89
Yes	11

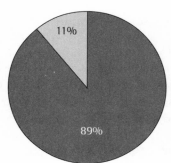

If Yes, Which One?

	Total
	PERCENT
He	17
She	67
Both	16

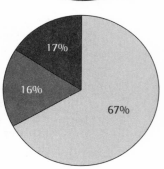

Eleven percent of our newlyweds profess that at least one of them was a virgin when they got married. Of those 11 percent, only 16 percent of the couples told us they *both* were virgins when they married.

Virginity is increasingly in vogue today, compared to when I got married. The numbers of virgins dropped rapidly throughout the sixties, seventies, and eighties, but now, near the end of the nineties, our research shows that the trend is reversing and the number (11 percent) will probably continue to increase, almost but not quite back to the percentages that existed in the early part of the century.

Did You Have Sex on Your Wedding Night?

In the new category of "old before your time" or "honey, I shrunk myself into exhaustion," 32 percent of the newlyweds told us they did *not* have sex on their wedding night . . . mainly because they were too exhausted.

While newlyweds of *all* ages were tired, the most tired were the over-40 group (they must have stayed up past 10 P.M.). Those who were getting married for the second, third, or fourth time were the least likely to let fatigue win the day—or night!

Did You Wait Until After Marriage to Sleep Together?

	Total
	PERCENT
No	90
Yes	10

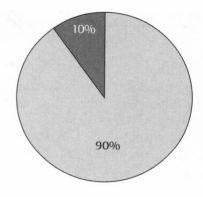

Don't show this one to Mom and Dad! Only 10 percent of our newlywed cóuples said they waited until they were married to sleep together. Those who waited for the big night were likely to be in the youngest group (18 to 24 years old), getting married for the first time, high school educated, and earning low incomes.

A scant 6 percent of those who were getting married for the *second* time told us they waited until *this* marriage was a done deal to consummate it.

On Average, How Often Did You Make Love on Your Honeymoon?

	Total	
		PERCENT
Times per Day		
≈ One		34
▫ Two		30
⬚ Three		20
■ Four		6
☐ Five		4
■ Six to Nine		3
Ten or more		1 couple only
▨ Zero		3

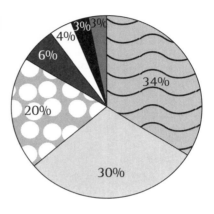

The most prolific lovemakers are young, with low incomes and less schooling, and, by a slight margin, are married for the first time.

For statistics lovers, the overall average was 2.28 times a day. But 3 percent told us they did not make love at all on their honeymoon. We can't fathom why. On the other end of the continuum are the 3 percent who told us they did it six to nine times a day—and the one pair who swear they did it 12 times a day. I got tired just typing in that answer!

I marvel at this 12-times-a-day couple and state that, as far as I can remember, my wife and I did it 12 times during the honeymoon and the first month combined. My younger daughter, the most recent newlywed in our family, would not answer this question, but she assures me her answers are among this book's statistics. That's fine by me; I really don't want to know any more than that.

Did You Carry Your Bride Over the Threshold When You Returned from the Honeymoon?

	Total
	PERCENT
No	66
Yes	34

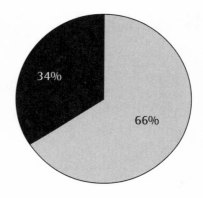

Another tradition bites the dust! Only 34 percent of the newly-wed wives were carried over the threshold when they first came back from the honeymoon. Another interesting aspect of the answers shows that more than half the men *forgot* that they had carried their wives across the threshold. When asked, they couldn't remember!

Among the remaining traditionalists, the majority are men ages 25 to 34 who earn more than $50,000 and are college-educated first-time husbands. Incidentally, we did find that 70 percent of the men married three or more times were also likely to continue this tradition.

Did Your Parents Oppose or Support Your Marriage?

	Total
	PERCENT
Supported Marriage	93
Opposed Marriage	7

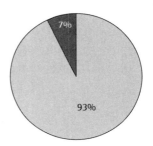

If Opposed, Why?

	Total
	PERCENT
Didn't Like Him/Her	24
Racial Difference	33
Religious Reason	43

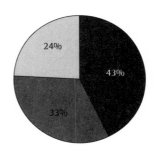

If the Reason Was Religious, Did One Party Offer to Convert?

	Total
	PERCENT
No	89
Yes	11

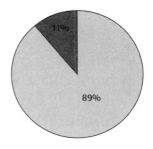

Of the 7 percent of parents who opposed a marriage, 24 percent said it was because they just didn't like the choice of the spouse and 43 percent cited religious reasons. Racial differences made up the remaining 33 percent of those families who opposed a specific partner.

As you might suspect, the biggest objection to a marriage came from the parents of those who were tying the knot for the third time or more: Nearly 20 percent of these newlyweds did not get an OK from their parents.

When You Slept Together for the First Time, Did Your Partner Meet Your Expectations?

	Total
	PERCENT
Yes	87
No	13

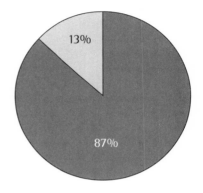

What a relief! Nearly everyone was satisfied with their spouse the first time they slept together. The 13 percent who felt their partner did not meet their expectations said the lovemaking has become better since then—great testimony to the importance of communication.

2
Now That You're Married

Did You Have Sex More Before Marriage or After?

	Total
	PERCENT
Before	67
After	33

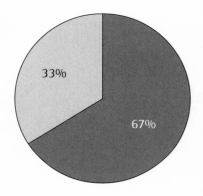

Can you imagine asking or answering this question 10 or 15 years ago? Sixty-seven percent of our newlywed couples tell us they had more sex *before* they were married than they do now, and they haven't even been married a year yet.

Those who had more sex *before* marriage are usually 18 to 24 years old, earn $30,000 to $49,000, have a high school education, and are married for the first time.

Do You Find Lovemaking Is
Better Now That You Are Married?

	Total
	PERCENT
No	28
Yes	72

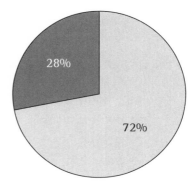

Almost three out of four newlyweds tell us they made love more often before they were married but their lovemaking is better since they got married. The quality has improved while the quantity has decreased. So here's to quality time!

The newlyweds who experienced the most improved lovemaking (as graded by themselves) are the college-educated, 25-to-34-year-olds, who earn $50,000 to $74,000 annually. Those married three or more times also gave themselves greatly improved lovemaking scores.

What One Thing Did You Let Your Spouse See or Do or Know Only After You Were Married?

The things we do in love. Read them, laugh, and relate.

burping	farting
my naked body in light	the spots on my arms
he bathes me	dentures
masturbating	walking around naked
my temper	my sexual fantasy
pictures of when I was fat	more of my feelings
crying	going to the bathroom in front of me
worrying	changing tampons
picking each other's pimples	me without makeup
my laziness	that I have bad gas

Best answer: "I introduced her to my imaginary friend."

What Are Your Spouse's
Best and Worst Qualities?

BEST	WORST
loyal	irresponsible
unselfish	forgetful
sexy	smelly feet
good personality	too neat
very understanding	bad temper
good in bed	procrastinator
always sexual	bitches too much
cares about others	passing gas
easy to talk to	leaves the toilet seat up
very loud	obnoxious
sense of humor	moody
protective nature	doesn't pick up stuff
very loving	too involved in sports
honest	total slob
faithful	eats too much
witty	dirty
nice-looking	selfish
his penis	smokes too much
patient	exaggerates
his butt	always interrupting me
her butt	possessive

BEST	WORST
her breasts	high-strung
tall and handsome	pouting
giving	anal personality
compassionate	teases me
listening	snores
sensitive	stubbornness
lovemaking	nose and ears
intelligent	big stomach
affectionate	his mouth
pampers me	domination
shows love	too serious
	lack of confidence
	no willpower
	gets mad easily
	crybaby
	sex only when he wants it
	can't read lips

Which qualities listed here match those of *your* mate?

What Is the Most Unusual
Way You Pamper Your Spouse?

Do we have the most wonderful, understanding, considerate newlyweds you ever heard of? Look at what they do to pamper their mates.

bathe him/her	full-body massage
massage feet	try to sense his needs
clean up for her	clean his ears
bake brownies	buy gifts for no reason
take him shopping for tools	talk baby talk
buy him a 12-pack	give him a bubble bath
give alcohol rubdowns	don't bitch
cut his nails	wash him/her after sex
rub/scratch his/her back	treat her like a tramp
bring breakfast in bed	buy clothes for him/her
give her money	sweet-talk him/her
cut her toenails	lick her all over
give in	brush her hair
give her a sponge bath	be nice to him
make love to her on demand	make Pop Tarts
talk dirty	trim his ear hairs
suck her toes	bring her flowers
scratch his back	shave his neck hair
put lotion on her back	rub her feet

pick dead skin off his toes

oral sex even though I hate it

polish her toenails

tie him up and give him fellatio
while wearing high heels and
a garter

do the dishes

lets me have my way

anything I want

pop the pimples on my back

give hugs and kisses

How Often Do You Tell Your Spouse "I Love You"?

	Total
	PERCENT
■ Daily	85
▤ A few times a week	9
▨ Once a week	2
■ Less than once a week	3
□ Never	1

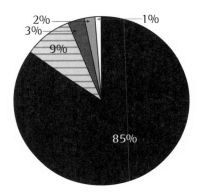

It strikes me as odd that 15 percent of these newlyweds don't say "I love you" every day. In fact, 1 percent told us they *never* say it. Now, I am not the greatest of great lovers, much to the surprise of only a few of you, but I say "I love you" every single day, and I have been married for almost 35 years. On the bright side, it may interest you to know that those married three or more times are the best at saying "I love you" every day (94 percent).

Those who don't say "I love you" much tend to be in the oldest group of newlyweds (over 40), with middle incomes and less education. Those married twice are also more guilty of not offering the words.

Do You Use the Bathroom at the Same Time?

	Total
	PERCENT
Yes	70
No	30

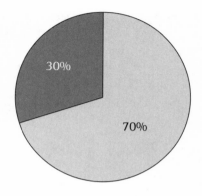

Seventy percent of married couples are sharing the bathroom, with those over 40 slightly more shy (58 percent). Not in our house. My wife doesn't care who's over, or if she is in Macy's window, she will share the bathroom with me or anyone else around.

For those married for the first time, the answer was 64 percent, while 84 percent of newlyweds married for the third time answered yes. Those people practically live in the bathroom together!

Younger couples with lower incomes and less education are more apt to share the bathroom than the higher-income, better-educated couples. Does this tell us anything?

Does Your Husband Leave the Toilet Seat Up More Often Than Not?

	Total
	PERCENT
Yes	27
No	73

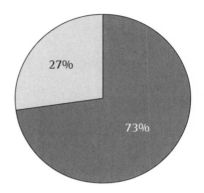

This is not only a question for newlyweds. Interestingly enough, more men admitted to this dreadful deed (35 percent) than the women who (at 24 percent) said it is a habit that drives them crazy.

The men most likely to have this habit are those with incomes of less than $30,000. Forty-four percent of these men are apt to be leaver-uppers, while the wealthier group of men are least likely, at only 11 percent, to do this. What does this tell us? Perhaps those earning less are more in a hurry, while the wealthy have more time on their hands.

Men married twice are more guilty than those married only once, and those married three or more times are even more guilty than the twice-married.

Do You Set Aside Time in Your Day to Talk Together?

	Total
	PERCENT
Yes	76
No	24

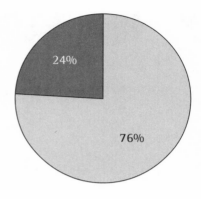

Communication! It appears that not all newlyweds are with the program. The success of a marriage is built on communication, and yet 24 percent of our newlyweds don't set aside time in their day to do just that.

A word from the wise to that 24 percent: Change your act. Communication will certainly improve and protect your marriage.

The couples that need most to communicate are mostly 25 to 34, with an income of less than $30,000 a year and a high school education.

How Many Times a Day Do You Call Each Other from Work?

	Total	
	PERCENT	
■ None	10	
□ Once	33	
■ Twice	26	
▤ Three Times	18	
≈ Four or more	13	

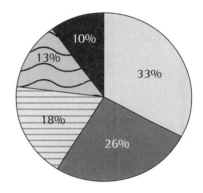

Newlyweds can't seem to get enough of each other even when they are apart. Many spend the company's money on telephone calls at least twice a day, 18 percent doing it three times and 13 percent calling four or more times daily. We have couples who call each other 10 or 20 times a day because they miss each other so much. The most talkative of all are in the youngest group (18 to 24 years old), who are obviously still very much on their honeymoon.

My daughters tell me their husbands call them at least three times a day from the car phone. How did we ever live before cellular phones?

Now That You Are Married, Who Is More Romantic?

	He Says	She Says
	PERCENT	PERCENT
He	38	23
She	24	31
Equal	38	46

This is a "he said he" and "she said she" answer. The men claim they are more romantic, while the women boast they are more romantic by far. Nearly half of the newlywed couples say they are equally romantic. The bottom line is that by a very slight margin (29 percent vs. 26 percent) the women win.

Looking at the results by age, we find that younger men (18 to 24) are slightly more romantic than their wives. But the other age groups clearly tell us that the women are more romantic.

For couples married three times or more, however, the man is the more romantic by far.

My wonderful newlywed daughter and her husband say, "We both share the romance." They have a jar full of romance ideas (i.e., BUY FLOWERS, WRITE A LOVE NOTE) in their home. Each Sunday they pick one out and surprise the other over the following week. This way they keep the romance alive. What a great idea for newlyweds—or even us long-timers.

Do You Kiss Good-Bye Before
You Leave for the Day?

	Total
	PERCENT
No	11
Yes	89

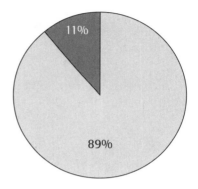

It's nice to know that no matter how old we get (35+), how much we earn (75K+), and how many times we marry (three+), we still keep the newlywed romance alive. Eighty-nine percent of those surveyed plant one on the smacker on their way out for the day.

Do You Have Nicknames for Each Other?

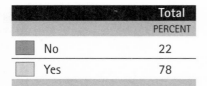

	Total
	PERCENT
No	22
Yes	78

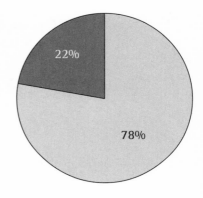

We are a nickname society. Nearly everyone among our newly-weds has a nickname. Here's a sampling:

Poopie	Coach	Muffy
Honey	Sweetheart	Pumpkin
Kid	Dopeyhead	Big Bear
Smokey	Mr. Smith	Moron
Babe	Liver lips	Woman
Boy	Pook	Sweetie
Lovey	Silly	Honeybunch
Will	Taffy	Baby
Boo	Little girl	Big guy
Cowboy	Horny honey	Cutie
Babycakes	Handsome man	Pretty lady
Snuggle muffin	Sweet pea	Sillyhead
Crazy	Kat	Turkey
Honey bunny	Redman	Wiggle butt
Cutie	Babykins	Beermeister
Pooh bear	Sugar woogum	Fuzzy butt
Babydoll	My chick	My life, my love
Squishy fuzzy	Buddha	Kitten
Hooter	Baby doll	Pussycat
Pokey	Blondie	Putz
Frisky	Cupcake	Johnson
Sweetmeat	Honeypie	Bubba

What Was the Real Reason You Married Your Spouse?

	Total*
	PERCENT
Love	89
Companionship	41
Pregnant	6
Lonely	4
Money	1
Combinations of above	8

*Adds to more than 100 percent due to multiple answers

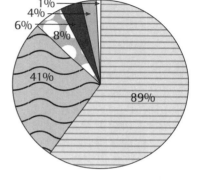

Love still seems to be the main best reason for getting married these days. I am more than a bit surprised at the number of those who say they married for companionship, loneliness, or money.

You might find it interesting to know that the majority of those respondents marrying for money or companionship were men.

Have You Ever Regretted Getting Married?

	Total	Men	Women
	PERCENT	PERCENT	PERCENT
No	91	99	87
Yes	9	*	13

*Fewer than 1 percent of respondents

Looks like there is potential trouble here. Though married less than one year, 9 percent of the newlyweds have already regretted their decision at least once. Yet virtually everyone stating the regret was a woman!

These female respondents are younger (18 to 24 years old), earn less than $30,000 a year, and are high school educated. Unfortunately, many of the second- and third-time-married women also felt the same way.

Let's hope they all give it time to straighten out their problems and become part of the 91 percent who seem happy with their marriage decision and with life in general.

What Activities Do You Like to Do Together the Best?

Following are the more popular things newlyweds like to do together. They are listed in order of the most frequently cited.

going to the movies

having sex

dining out

shopping

watching TV

playing sports

traveling

walking

golfing

dancing

riding bikes

playing tennis

camping

being with friends

going to church

swimming

fishing

sharing romantic evenings

playing pool

renting movies

going to concerts

drinking

cooking

What Does Your Spouse Do That You Despise?

Get ready for another outpouring of things that just plain upset newlywed spouses. Here is a sample.

watching sports on TV

going to a relative's house

buying tools

having obnoxious friends

going out drinking

going to his mom's house

eating weird oriental dishes

watching X-rated videos

eating dead skin from his feet

going out with the guys

spitting out the car window

chewing tobacco

having an obsession with guns

placing wet towels on top of dry clothes

shopping

talking on the phone constantly

complaining about my mother's calls

visiting friends in the middle of the night

ignoring me

telling my ex to stay away

leaving the house and not coming back for hours

getting mad as hell

erasing phone messages from my friends

thinking about killing my ex

not talking to me for a week

crying at the slightest thing

calling me names

hiding in the bedroom closet

being overprotective

having no sex for a week as punishment if I don't do what she wants

going to bed with my best friend before we were married

calling an ex-girlfriend of mine and telling her I only used her for sex

getting us thrown out of a bar

Most upsetting comment of all: "Does the name Lorena Bobbitt mean anything? She threatens!"

What One Thing About Your Spouse Do You Wish You Could Change?

Since all newlyweds are perfect for and to each other, this is a very short list. It will grow as they spend more time together.

make his ears smaller

cure his alcohol problem

get him to pick up his clothes

make him/her more romantic

give me more affection

stop snoring

control his/her temper

stubbornness

mood swings

PMS

work fewer hours

spend less money

have more sex

have much more sex

have much, much more sex

never say no

say yes sometimes

let me be right sometimes

And then there were the respondents who wrote, "Nothing. I love him (her) just the way he (she) is."

Do Your Friends Like Your Spouse?
Do You Like Your Spouse's Friends?

	Total	Total
	PERCENT	PERCENT
	Friends Like Spouse	Like Spouse's Friends
Yes	97	91
No	3	9

Thank God! Two fewer things to argue about. It seems things are OK with friends in all directions, yours, mine, and ours!

A few women did admit to faking affection for their spouse's friends in order to spare his feelings. In the other (small) instance, both the friends *and* the spouse were aware when they were disliked.

Do You Wear a Wedding Ring?

	Total	Men	Women
	PERCENT	PERCENT	PERCENT
Yes	86	74	93
No	14	26	7

Eighty-six percent of our couples wear a wedding ring. The number would be higher if all the men would cooperate. Only 74 percent told us they wear the beloved wedding ring, compared to 93 percent of the women.

My ring never comes off. My newlywed daughter says her husband tried the old "I never wear jewelry; what if my fingers swell?" routine. But when it came down to it, he was happy to wear his ring and never takes it off either. If he tries to, she will kill him!

Men over 40, earning the big dollars and married more than once, are the culprits who won't wear a ring. As for the young (18 to 24) and in love, it is almost a done deal. In 98 percent of these marriages, both partners wear a ring to signify their togetherness.

Do You Spend More Time with Your Own Friends or with Your Spouse's Friends?

	Men	Women
	PERCENT	PERCENT
Own Friends	20	73
Spouse's Friends	80	27

The results indicate that men are spending most of their time with "her" friends. He says so (80 percent), and she says so (73 percent).

If you are one of the few wives who finds herself spending more time with "his" friends, you are likely to be 18 to 24 years old and probably very lonely for "your" friends.

Has Your Spouse Gone on Vacations Without You Since the Wedding?

	Total	He Says	She Says
	PERCENT	PERCENT	PERCENT
No, my spouse stays with me	80	77	85
Yes, my spouse has vacationed without me	20	23	15

And you thought it was a man's world! Even though these newlyweds are barely past the honeymoon, more women than men have already gone on a separate vacation.

The women who are on the loose tend to be over 40, married more than once, and college educated.

In all the years I have been married, I have never been on vacation alone. My wife just won't give me permission to do it. Maybe I should let her go, because she also has a perfect record of zero vacations without me.

How Often Do You Speak to Your Parents, Now That You Are Married?

Times a Week	Total	He	She
	PERCENT	PERCENT	PERCENT
None	7	11	2
One or Two	44	38	47
Three or Four	14	20	9
Five or Six	5	13	2
Seven	29	18	38
More than Seven	1	0	2
Average	3.49	2.55	3.87

The average Mrs. speaks to her mom or dad 3.87 times a week, and 40 percent talk at least once a day. The average Mr., on the other hand, speaks with mom or dad fewer than three times a week, and 11 percent do so less than once a week.

Guys, you might want to keep an eye on the phone bill if you are among the lucky group whose wife is talking to mom or dad at least two times a *day*.

How Often Do You Speak to Your In-Laws?

		Total
		PERCENT
▰	As little as possible	3
▢	Once a week	58
☐	Twice a week	14
▤	Three times a week	10
▰	More than three times a week	15

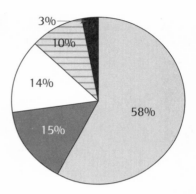

This question turned out to be a no-brainer. Virtually all who gave the answer "as little as possible" were men. But the opposite is true when it comes to the answer at the other end of the scale, MORE THAN THREE TIMES A WEEK. It is heavily weighted in favor of the daughter-in-law who does the dialing—though 6 percent of men do admit to talking with their in-laws at least three times a week.

Those well-intentioned females who speak with the in-laws most are those who are 40 and older.

What Do You Call Your In-Laws?

	Total*	Men	Women
	PERCENT	PERCENT	PERCENT
By First Name	70	69	70
Mom and Dad	34	48	26
Mr. and Mrs.	7	1	9

*Adds to more than 100 percent due to multiple answers

This question brings a mixed bag of replies, as attested to by my own experience with my sons-in-law, one for nearly 10 years and one a newlywed. The newlywed calls me Dad; however, my son-in-law of nearly 10 years avoided calling my wife and me anything specific for a while. When he'd phone he would say "Hi, it's Dave," rather than call us Mom and Dad or even use our names. Now, with three children of his own, he gets off easier by calling us Poppa and Grandma.

There is no right or wrong answer to this. It is not uncommon to find just about any kind of mix-and-match situation. The wife may call the father-in-law by his name but call the mother-in-law Mom, the husband may refer to both by name, and so on. The overriding answer from our newlyweds clearly shows that first names are the most popular.

Has Your Sex Life Become Routine Since You've Married?

	Total	Men	Women
	PERCENT	PERCENT	PERCENT
Yes	39	19	49
No	61	81	51

Doesn't it take two to tango? More than one-third say their sex life has become routine. This is bad enough for newlyweds, who have been married for such a short time, but what is more startling is that only 19 percent of the men seem to think it is routine but nearly half the women—49 percent—feel that way. What gives?

If you don't want your sex life to become routine, our newlyweds suggest trying any or all of the following:

new positions	baby oils and massages
bubble baths	tying each other up
different places	sex toys
sex in the car	role-playing
fantasizing	waiting a few days to do it

Now That You Are Married, Who Usually Initiates Lovemaking More?

	He Says	She Says
	PERCENT	PERCENT
He	60	50
She	22	16
Equal	18	34

Hurrah for the nineties woman! While I suspected that men would instigate lovemaking more often, it is heartening to know that 22 percent of women are firmly in charge and more than 30 percent are equally as assertive in this area as their new husbands.

Our data show that female initiators cross all age groups and income levels but are found more often among high school graduates. We need to help college-educated women get with the program.

Now That You're Married, Who Is More Aggressive During Lovemaking?

	He Says	She Says
	PERCENT	PERCENT
He	55	42
She	18	22
Equal	27	36

The macho-man image comes to mind with this question, as both men and women agree that the man is more aggressive when it comes to lovemaking. However, it is comforting that women are not far behind. Almost 25 percent of all women claim to be just as aggressive as their partners.

The most aggressive men are 18 to 24 years old, earn less than $30,000 a year, and have a college education. Among the most aggressive women, the average is 18 to 24 years old, first time married, in a family that earns $30,000 to $49,000 a year, and with a high school education.

Do You Fantasize About Others Besides Your Spouse?

	Total	Men	Women
	PERCENT	PERCENT	PERCENT
No	78	67	82
Yes	22	33	18

If Yes, Do You Tell Your Spouse About the Fantasies?

	Total	Men	Women
	PERCENT	PERCENT	PERCENT
No	54	49	62
Yes	46	51	38

Do You Tell Your Spouse About the People in Your Fantasies?

	Total	Men	Women
	PERCENT	PERCENT	PERCENT
No	69	61	78
Yes	31	39	22

Newlywed men are the fantasizers in the family, and do they like to talk about it! More men have fantasies about someone other than their spouse, they tell their wives about the fantasies, and they even name the people they are fantasizing about. Does that sound like trouble or what? Women, I'm sure you want to know who the most likely fantasizers are. Well, they are ages 25 to 34 and earn less than $30,000 a year.

Do You Both Work?

	Total
	PERCENT
No	23
Yes	77

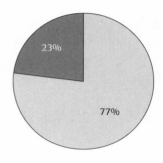

If Yes, Do You Have a Joint or a Separate Bank Account or Both?

	Total
	PERCENT
Joint	60
Separate	15
Both	25

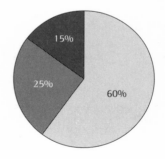

The answer to this question is truly the new word of the decade: DINKs! What are DINKs? They're the newlyweds of the nineties: *D*ual *I*ncome, *N*o *K*ids. Seventy-seven percent are in this category. The ones who don't work are in the youngest category (18 to 24 years old), with family income under $30,000 a year.

As for banking, most—60 percent—have a joint account; however, 15 percent go it separately, and 25 percent have both joint and separate accounts.

3
Before and After

How Many Times a Day Did You Have a Loving Thought About Your Spouse Before You Were Married?

	Total	Men	Women
	PERCENT	PERCENT	PERCENT
Times			
1–3	16	22	12
4–6	18	21	17
7–10	23	20	25
More than 10	43	37	46
Average	17.5	13.9	18.9

How Many Times a Day Do You Have a Loving Thought About Your Spouse Now?

	Total	Men	Women
	PERCENT	PERCENT	PERCENT
Times			
1–3	21	22	20
4–6	22	16	25
7–10	31	47	24
More than 10	26	15	31
Average	12.8	9.8	13.7

Both men and women have fewer loving thoughts about their partners once they are wearing a band of gold. For both sexes, the numbers dropped by roughly 37 percent.

How Often Do You Kiss?

	Before Marriage	After Marriage
	PERCENT	PERCENT
Every day	90	91
A few times a week	10	6
Less than once a week	—	3

Ninety-one percent of our newlyweds keep up the good work. Nearly 10 percent of newlyweds, however, don't kiss every day, either before or after marriage. Yikes! Luckily, those who kissed only a few times a week dropped from 10 percent prior to marriage to 6 percent once married.

I'm thankful my married daughters are within the norm for this answer. They tell me they still smooch daily with their spouses.

A word to the wise comes from those twice- and thrice-marrieds who learned their lessons: They are everyday kissers!

Which of the Following Describes Your Real Feelings About Your Engagement Ring?

| | Total |
	PERCENT
It's just what I wanted	72
It's not what I wanted, but I can live with it	11
Wow! It's huge	10
It's so tiny . . .	2
Wait, where is it? Huh, I'm not getting one?	5

Does it surprise you that, all in all, 18 percent of the women were a bit taken aback by the appearance of their ring? "It's not what I wanted, but I can live with it" said 11 percent of the women, 5 percent had a tough time finding it, proclaiming, "Wait, where is it?" and another 2 percent plain out said, "It's so tiny."

Only 10 percent of the men seemed to have spent too much money, as their honeys said, "Wow! It's huge."

Were you a grateful recipient? Men, did you do the right thing? Just ask your wife . . . if you dare!

Did You Observe Valentine's Day Before Your Marriage? Do You Still Observe It?

	Total
	PERCENT
Before	
No	16
Yes	84
After	
No	4
Yes	96

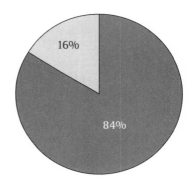

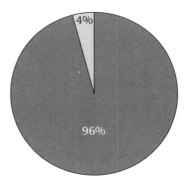

Cupid is alive and well! Eighty-four percent of the newlyweds observed Valentine's Day *before* they were married, and the figure climbs to a whopping 96 percent after the vows were swapped. What a great testimony to everlasting love.

Who Talks on the Phone More?

	Total
	PERCENT
He	28
She	72

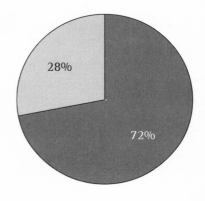

Reaching out and touching someone is attributed to one sex overwhelmingly. I can't believe that 28 percent of newlywed men actually talk more than their women. In my home it is 99.9 percent for the wife and 0.1 percent for me.

My daughters have followed in the footsteps of their mother. Both control the phones in their respective homes by a wide margin.

Do You Agree on What TV Shows to Watch?

Sixty-five percent of our newlyweds agree on what to watch; the remaining 35 percent either fight about it or one goes to another room.

Who Controls the Remote?

What is becoming of my fellowman in this world? Would you believe that only 85 percent of husbands hold on to the remote control? How can it be that 15 percent of wives can actually commandeer the one thing in life that I believe is rightfully a man's possession?

Who are these women? I did everything I could to track them down and came up with the following profile:

She most likely lives in Connecticut, Alabama, Wyoming, or Illinois.

She is probably over 35.

She is in a big-time-earning home, over $75,000.

She has been married more than once.

Do You Shower Together?
How Often Do You Make Love in the Shower?

I asked these questions of the general public for the book *Do You Do It with the Lights On?* and found that 94 percent of couples showered together. I expected the numbers would be even higher among our very sexy newlyweds. Instead, we found that only 67 percent shower together.

Love in the shower is *not* a practice of 53 percent of newlyweds; they just don't seem to have time. Thirty-five percent did tell us they do it once a week, and 12 percent find time to do it more frequently.

Do You Fall Asleep Holding Each Other?

	Total	Men	Women
	PERCENT	PERCENT	PERCENT
Yes	61	42	68
No	39	58	32

Holding is good: enjoyable, sexy, comforting, and fun! Nearly two-thirds (61 percent) tell us they do it. But it appears that the men are already sleeping. Only 42 percent seem to remember whether they do it or not, while nearly 70 percent of the women are confident they are cuddling.

Which Best Describes Your Sleeping Position?

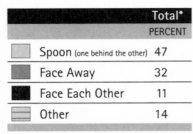

	Total*
	PERCENT
Spoon (one behind the other)	47
Face Away	32
Face Each Other	11
Other	14

* Adds to more than 100 percent due to multiple answers

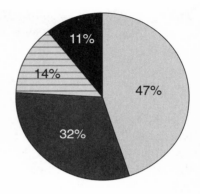

Men and women newlyweds agree that spooning is the in thing. But what are the 14 percent who said they sleep in the OTHER positions doing?

Now That You Are Married, Do You Surprise Your Spouse with a Gift More or Less Often Than When You Were Dating?

	Total	Men	Women
	PERCENT	PERCENT	PERCENT
More Often	40	38	42
Less Often	60	62	58

Those lovely surprise gifts people received when they were dating have slowed down significantly. Sixty percent give fewer gifts now that they are married.

The thoughtful 40 percent who give more surprise gifts as newly-weds are most likely to be the older set (over 40) who earn between $50,000 and $74,000 a year and who are married for the third time or more.

My newlywed daughter is happy to say that her marriage defies the odds—they definitely give as many gifts, if not more, now they are married.

Have You Gained Weight Since
You First Met Your Spouse?

	Total	Men	Women
	PERCENT	PERCENT	PERCENT
No	21	17	23
Yes	79	83	77

How About Your Spouse?

	Total	Men	Women
	PERCENT	PERCENT	PERCENT
No	29	19	40
Yes	71	81	60

All that wining and dining sure takes a toll on the waistline! Seventy-nine percent of our newlyweds admit to putting on the pounds. When we asked about the spouse, 81 percent of men felt their wife is more woman than she was when they married. Only 60 percent of women felt their husbands were doing some growing of their own.

Where Is Your Wedding Gown Now?

	Total
	PERCENT
Attic	56
Cleaners	25
Lent it out	5
Who knows?	14

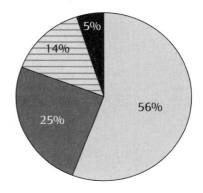

Having paid for two very expensive weddings, I sure hope neither of my daughters answers "Who knows?" as did 14 percent of our newlywed females.

Lending out your wedding gown during the year following the wedding seems as if it should be against some kind of rule. Nonetheless, 5 percent have done it.

4
Sex, Sex, and More Sex

I devised the matrix of statistical data I call "Sex, sex, and more or less sex in a new marriage" by asking the newlyweds to tell us how often they had sex before marriage and how often during months 1, 6, and 12 (the last category only for those married that long). We added the figures up, divided by days, weeks, and months, and came up with something that looks like this:

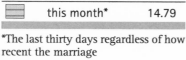

Sex Per Month	
	NUMBER OF TIMES
■ Before Marriage	31.77
After Marriage	
▢ month one	29.48
▨ month six	19.80
⠿ month twelve	16.72
▤ this month*	14.79

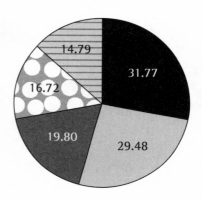

*The last thirty days regardless of how recent the marriage

You don't have to be a genius to understand this table. I nearly had a heart attack just reading it. (Remember, I have been married almost 35 years.) Before marriage, couples were doing it more than once a day, but the frequency drops at each interval. Now it is around once every two days. What will it be in 35 years? I'll never tell! Let them wait and see.

Here are a few interesting sidelights, highlights, and lowlights to the data.

Thirty percent told us that before marriage, they were doing it a few times a day. Imagine! Well, these same people have worn themselves out, as only 13 percent are still doing it a few times a day after less than a year of marriage.

Everybody was doing it at least once a week before they were married, and now would you believe we have 5 percent who do it less than once a week, 2 percent who do it a few times a month, 2 percent who do it less than once a month, and 3 percent who do it even less frequently?

Do you think men exaggerate? Before marriage, men told us they did it 35 times a month while women did it 26 times. (Men must be doing it themselves and counting it toward their totals.)

As of today, these same men tell us they are still doing it 24 times a month while the wives are doing it 13 times. At least the men are consistent.

The most active (lovemaking wise, that is) couples are the youngest, the high school educated, and those who don't earn much annually. Those who seem to be the fastest to lose interest are mostly women who are over 40, have a middle-range income, and are college educated.

Did You Masturbate Before You Were Married? Do You Masturbate Now?

	Men		Women	
	PERCENT		PERCENT	
	Before	After	Before	After
No	27	63	52	60
Yes	73	37	48	40

Some of you may remember when the Surgeon General of the United States left the job shortly after discussing this subject in relation to schools and teenagers in late 1994.

According to our survey, more than half of the newlywed adults did this before marriage, with the percentage falling to just slightly below 50 percent after marriage. So it's obvious a whole lot of folks masturbate as part of a seemingly happy sex life.

Different strokes for different folks!

Do You Do Things Sexually Now That You Didn't Do Before You Got Married?

	Total	He	She
	PERCENT	PERCENT	PERCENT
No	62	75	53
Yes	38	25	47

A very healthy 38 percent of newlyweds have done some new and, we hope, exciting things to spice up their sex lives. When we look at the answers, however, we come up with a statistical quirk. Only 25 percent of the men say they are doing something new, but nearly twice as many women (47 percent) say they are doing something new! It makes you wonder.

Now for the good stuff. Here is a partial list of what new things our respondents have done sexually since their wedding:

perform oral sex	make love outdoors
touch more in tender spots	experiment more
tie each other up	watch porno movies
have sex in an unusual place	dress up
masturbate each other	use vibrators
use sex toys	talk dirty
become more aggressive	have anal sex

Looking at the details of the statistics, we find the more experimental women are 25 to 34 years old and in the middle-income range ($30K to $49K per year).

How Many Sexual Partners Have You Had in Your Entire Life?

How Many Sexual Partners Would You Say Your Partner Has Had?

	He Says*	She Says*
I've had	10	12
Spouse has had	18	8

*Average numbers

The answer to this question is in my opinion the most stunning in the whole survey. In both instances the women were said to have had more sexual partners. This was stated by both the men and the women, who were asked separately.

It is equally noteworthy that while the men said they had had 10 partners, their own wives guessed it was 8. Pretty close; off only by two. However, the men thought their wives had had an average of 18 partners while the women admitted to only 12—quite a difference.

Does strength in numbers count? We have a few very "loving" people in our survey: 5 percent of both women and men told us they had had more than 40 partners. However, while 1 percent of the women told us they had had more than 100 sexual partners, we did not find a single man claiming more than 46. When it comes to guesswork, the imagination runs even wilder: 2 percent of women and 4 percent of men told us their partners had more than 100 partners.

Does Your Spouse Basically Know Everything About Your Sexual Past?

	Total
	PERCENT
Yes	79
No	21

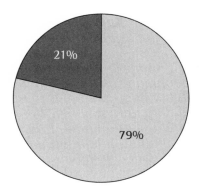

21%

79%

Of our newlyweds, 21 percent keep a sexual secret from their spouse. "Mum's the word" applies most often to men and women in the 25-to-34-year-old group who earn more than $75,000 a year and are college educated. Those married more than three times also have a host of secrets, which include:

names, names, names
frequency of sex
number of partners
what I did
where I did it
who didn't satisfy me
I had an abortion
making love to his cousin before we got married
making love to her maid of honor on the wedding day
having a venereal disease before we met
having oral sex with someone other than my husband
making love with two men at the same time
sleeping with her mother

What's On, Sometimes or Always, When You Make Love?

	Total*
	PERCENT
Lights	44
TV	31
Radio	37
Other	23

*Adds up to more than 100 percent due to multiple answers

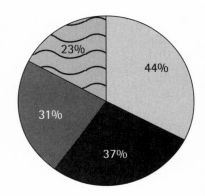

Lights on while making love appears to be more a female thing than a male thing (51 percent vs. 35 percent). Likewise, the women are more adventurous in the OTHER category (30 percent vs. 20 percent), which includes candles, ceiling fans, and the stereo turned down low to play soft music. Older (40+) women love to make love with the lights on, more so than any other age group. When we look at the number of times married, those married three or more times also like the lights on much more than any other group.

More men prefer the TV and radio on than do women, by a count of 43 percent to 29 percent. These men tend to be much younger (18 to 24). One man reported that his wife always has her socks on when making love. Cold feet?

If You Use a Condom, Who Puts It on Him?

	Total
	PERCENT
He Does	63
She Does	37

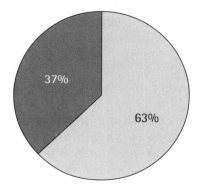

More than one-third of the women told us they are the condom appliers in the family.

You might be interested to know that among the female set no one over 40 admits to doing this, while the under-$30,000 first-time-married high-school-educated women are the most practiced at it.

Do You Have to Be Kissed in Order to Make Love?

	Total	Men	Women
	PERCENT	PERCENT	PERCENT
Yes	36	43	30
No	64	57	70

I thought of this question because my wife refuses to make love if she is not kissed (even when she has a cold). I personally would rather miss a kiss than miss a session of lovemaking. So you can imagine how surprised I was when the results indicated that among newlyweds it is the man who needs to be kissed more than the woman.

At a recent party I asked the question of seven couples; without prompting, all the women raised their hands as if in class to say, "Yes, I have to be kissed!" As my friend Mel was leaving several hours later, he called out, "Thanks, now I'll have to kiss her when we do it tonight." The men who need to be kissed are likely to be 25 to 34 years old, married for the first time, earning $75,000 annually, and college educated. Men married three times also plead this case more often than others.

When Making Love, Do You Prefer to Be on Top or on the Bottom?

	Men	Women
	PERCENT	PERCENT
Top	54	45
Bottom	46	55

This is what I call the jockeying-for-position question. While the percentages are relatively close, both men and women generally like him on top.

We thought it would be interesting to look at who the reverse people are; that is, women who like the top and men who like the bottom. Any of these characteristics sound familiar?

WOMEN LIKING TOP	MEN LIKING BOTTOM
over 40	18 to 24
$50–74K	under $30K
high school educated	college educated
married three times	married two times

Who Talks More During Lovemaking?

	Total
	PERCENT
He	26
She	74

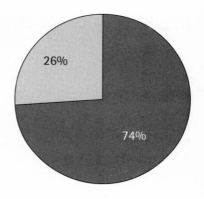

The results are in, and they overwhelmingly confirm that women do the talking during lovemaking; 74 percent told us they take charge verbally while making love, and the men confirmed it.

It was hard to find a profile of the most talkative female group because so many do it. But our trusty computer says they are young (18 to 24) and in a lower income bracket.

Do You Undress in Front of Your Mate?

	Total	Men	Women
	PERCENT	PERCENT	PERCENT
Yes	96	99	94
No	4	1	6

As the figures show, nearly every newlywed couple told us they undress in front of each other. One of the very few exceptions is the reluctance of some of the women in the 18-to-24-year-old group.

Many older people (65+) told us they had been married before for as long as 50 years and had never ever undressed in front of their former mate.

This directly contradicts my own experience. My wife and I have always undressed in front of each other. However, this doesn't make me feel particularly special. My wife will undress in front of anyone at any time. I must be careful or I will spy her in Bloomingdale's window one day.

Women: Do You Wear the Sexy Lingerie from Your Shower, or Does It Stay in the Closet?

	Total
	PERCENT
Wear It	64
Stays in Closet	36

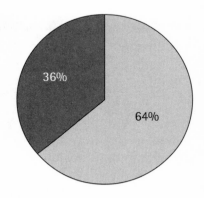

There are closets everywhere full of sexy lingerie that is gathering dust. While our data show that women of all ages are not wearing sexy lingerie, it is the older (over 40) women who are the least likely to wear it. Also, women who have been married more than once won't don the sexy lingerie.

And, in case you're wondering, the bridal showers where the lingerie was given were seldom a surprise. Seventy-eight percent of all brides-to-be had the date of the bridal shower circled on her calendar.

Have You Ever Asked Your Partner to Change Lovemaking Techniques? If Yes, Did It Happen?

	Total
	PERCENT
No	54
Yes	46

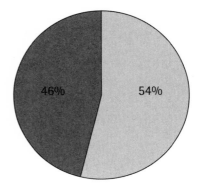

Lovemaking is surely an art in the nineties. Nearly half our newlyweds have asked their partners to change their technique, and we found the requests to be equally shared between men and women.

The "change," however, brought a whole different set of statistics. When the woman asked the man to change his technique, he obliged in 93 percent of the cases. But when the man asked his wife to change, only 62 percent went along with it.

Seems like our male respondents could use a course in persuasive speaking.

Do You Believe Your Spouse Has Been Unfaithful?

	Total	Men	Women
	PERCENT	PERCENT	PERCENT
Yes	10	5	13
No	90	95	87

Twice as many women as men think their partners have been unfaithful. These nervous newlyweds tend to be among the youngest group (18 to 24 years old), earn less than $30,000 a year, and have high school educations.

Have You Ever Made Love to a Sleeping Partner?

	Total	Men	Women
	PERCENT	PERCENT	PERCENT
No	69	69	69
Yes	31	31	31

This is an interesting question you may have thought of at one time or another, but has it ever been asked of you?

If Yes, Did You Finish or Did Your Partner Awaken?

	Total	Men	Women
	PERCENT	PERCENT	PERCENT
Awakened	86	80	88
Completed	14	20	12

Those sex therapists out there may be able to help me with this one: Exactly the same percentage of men and women admit to trying this deed. And, going one step further, 14 percent actually completed what they started while their partner was asleep. Needless to say, more men claim to have done this than women. I'm not sure I understand how women can do this successfully, but I hope everyone is having fun.

Do You Go to the Bathroom Before Having Sex?

	Total
	PERCENT
Yes	56
No	44

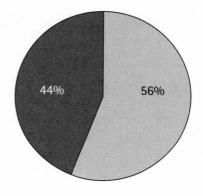

Spontaneity is dwindling for more than half of our newlyweds; 56 percent tell us they use the bathroom before having sex. The response was about the same for everyone.

Do You Go to the Bathroom After Sex?

	Total
	PERCENT
Yes	87
No	13

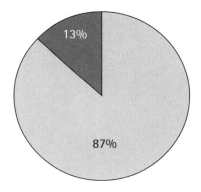

Toilets are flushing from coast to coast! It looks like just about everyone is headed for the bathroom after making love.

If You Have Sex in the Morning, Do You Brush Your Teeth First?

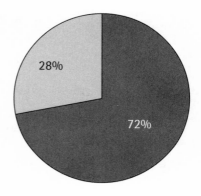

	Total
	PERCENT
Yes	28
No	72

My co-author daughter declares that both she and her husband hate "morning breath." Contrary to their feelings, only 28 percent of our respondents brush their teeth before morning loving. These are likely to be 25-to-34 first-time newlyweds, who earn $75,000 or more a year and are college educated.

Do You Brush Your Teeth Before a Plain Old Good-Morning Kiss?

More people get up to brush before making love (28 percent) than those who intend to have just a simple good-morning kiss (20 percent).

What Is Your Favorite Sexual Position?

How many ways do I love thee? We didn't know what to expect, and we were right.

sitting down on top of me

with my mother-in-law sleeping in the room

with him on the bottom

with my wife on the top

doggie style

with legs on his shoulders

sixty-nine

sixty-three

hips on pillow

lying down sideways

tied up

every way

any way

in a public place . . . standing up!

at work on the copier

in the boss's office on his desk when he goes home

number 26 in the sex book my mother bought me

back-to-back

at the movies, masturbating each other in the dark

Sick, sick, sick, and a lot of fun. Oh, those newlyweds!
Note to newlyweds: I sure hope you carry accident insurance.

What Is Your Favorite Place at Home to Make Love Other Than in the Bedroom?

Love comes in all shapes and sizes and amazing places within your own home.

living room couch	living room table
hallway stairs	living room floor
table	in front of the fireplace
swimming pool	kitchen
shower	antique bathtub
weight bench	pool deck
den	basement
pool table	roof
garage	in the car in the garage
bathroom	in the backyard

Have You Ever Made Love in Your Car?

	Total	Men	Women
	PERCENT	PERCENT	PERCENT
Yes	51	45	55
No	49	55	45

More women than men told us they had made love in the car (55 percent vs. 45 percent). Who are these very exciting and sexy women? They are newlyweds who are 18 to 24 years old, earn a household income of $50,000 to $75,000 annually, are college educated, and are married for the first time.

Have You Ever Made Love in the Car While Driving?

	Total	Men	Women
	PERCENT	PERCENT	PERCENT
Yes	14	26	10
No	86	74	90

Many more men are making love in the car while driving than women. These men appear to be 18 to 24 years old, earn $50,000 to $75,000 a year, are high school educated, and are very, very happy.

Do You Ever Fool Around While Driving?

	Total	Men	Women
	PERCENT	PERCENT	PERCENT
Yes	70	61	75
No	30	39	25

The majority of newlyweds like to fool around while driving. More than two-thirds of those surveyed admit to this deed, with women taking the lead over men.

Although many newlyweds do it, the most likely women are 18 to 24 years old, earn $50,000 to $75,000 a year, are married for the first time, and have a high school education.

Do You Practice Safe Sex?

	Total
	PERCENT
Yes	58
No	42

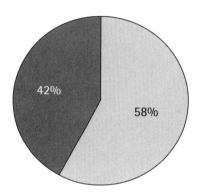

Have You Ever Been Tested for AIDS?

	Total
	PERCENT
Yes	51
No	49

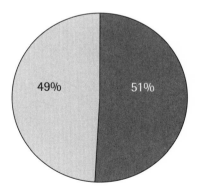

In this day and age, with all those life-threatening diseases going around, I'm surprised by the number of newlyweds who have never been tested for AIDS.

Don't you think an AIDS test should be mandatory before marriage? Isn't this in the best interests of both parties?

When Do You Plan to Start a Family?

	Total
	PERCENT
■ 0–6 months	27
⚃ 7–12 months	12
▢ More than 1 year	33
▤ Not sure	16
■ Never	12

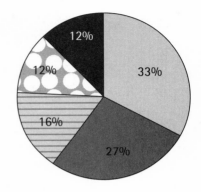

Sixty-one percent of our newlyweds say they are not planning to start a family for at least a year. Twelve percent indicate that they do not plan to have any children, but this may be an anomaly in our data because many of the women who said this are over child-bearing age. The real number is probably about 4 percent.

5
All's Fair in Love and War

What Do You Fight About Most Often?

This list runs on and on, so we have limited it to the best of the top answers. See if your hot topics are among them.

having children	bossiness
cleaning the apartment	ironing and doing windows
channel surfing	his sleeping
money, money, money	his being lazy
sex, sex, sex	disrespect
family	ex-spouse
mutual friends	immaturity
going out	golf
staying in	drugs
in-laws	past relationships
his friends	driving too fast
her friends	bills
drinking too much	leisure time
working too much	her cats
not socializing enough	lying
weight	cars
jealousy	trust

Do You Ever Go to Sleep Mad at Each Other?

	Total
	PERCENT
Yes	46
No	54

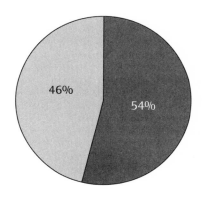

Priests, ministers, rabbis, and others who perform marriages always say, "No matter what happens during the day, you should never go to sleep without making up." So it's surprising that nearly half our newlyweds told us that in the brief time they have been married they will go to sleep when angry.

My newlywed daughter says this is one of the lessons she remembers learning from her parents. No matter what, she and her husband never go to sleep mad at each other. So, newlyweds, get with it! Nothing can be so important that you can't resolve your differences before you go to sleep.

Do You Fight Over Room Temperatures?

	Total
	PERCENT
No	70
Yes	30

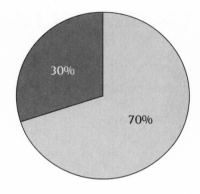

More men than women (38 percent vs. 24 percent) fight over the temperature in the house. The male fighters are usually the 18-to-24 set.

Men like it colder by a margin of 79 percent to 65 percent.

Our medical sources say this makes sense, since physiologically men have higher body temperatures.

Now That You Are Married, Who Says "I'm Sorry" First?

	He Says	She Says
	PERCENT	PERCENT
He	44	25
She	25	19
Equal Share	31	56

Both sexes say it is the man who is the first to break down and say he is sorry. Although the men seem more eager to take the blame, the women are quick to say that this could be an equal choice. A few men told us they try to hold out as long as possible. One man even held out for four days, while another told us it took him more than one week.

Women who have been married more than once say they are sorry first.

Who Yells Louder in a Fight?
Who Breaks More Things?

	Total	Men	Women
	PERCENT	PERCENT	PERCENT
Yells Louder			
He	32	46	24
She	68	54	76
Breaks More Things			
He	34	44	28
She	66	56	44

Whatever happened to sugar and spice and everything nice? The wives tend to have the tempers and yell louder. I guess that's why we guys apologize quicker!

How Do You Get Along with Your In-Laws?

	Total	Men	Women
	PERCENT	PERCENT	PERCENT
Great	54	39	66
Fair	36	47	26
Poor	4	*	7
Not at all	6	14	1

*Fewer than 1 percent of respondents

The answers to this question remind me of the famous quote from the Paul Newman movie, *Cool Hand Luke:* "What we have here is a failure to communicate."

Women say their relationship with their in-laws is really great, while men say theirs might be closer to fair. In the interest of preserving my extended family's relationships, I have been told by my wife that we love everyone.

Does One of You Have an Ex Who Will Not Let Go?

	Total
	PERCENT
Yes	10
No	90

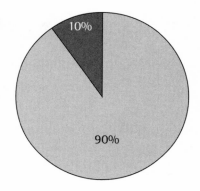

Only a small percentage of newlyweds report that an old flame or former spouse just won't go away. More men (14 percent) are still being pursued than women (9 percent).

We then asked those being pursued, "How often do you hear from the pursuer, and what is the most annoying or frightening thing your ex has ever done?"

There was no particular pattern in terms of timing for being pursued. It ranged from a few times a year all the way down to daily calls, with lots of combinations in between. We found, however, a myriad of excuses the exes use to bother the newlywed. The following is only a sample.

She called to tell us she was pregnant with my baby.

She wanted to beat up my wife.

She threatened to kill herself if I didn't come back.

He called just to say he was still alive.

She calls and hangs up when my wife picks up the phone.

He called police to our house for no reason other than to embarrass us.

Does Your Spouse Get Along with Your Mother?

	Total	Men	Women
	PERCENT	PERCENT	PERCENT
Yes	91	85	96
No	9	15	4

Surprise! Our newlyweds are off to a better-than-average start. Ninety-one percent say they get along great with their spouse's mother, although men don't seem to get along quite as well as the women do.

So if your husband is 18 to 24 years old, married for the first time, a high school graduate, and just starting to earn the bucks, beware. He may not get along too well with your mom.

6
Out on the Town

What Is the Most Annoying Thing
Your Mother-In-Law Does?

This question is one for the ages: The mother-in-law has been the butt of jokes for as long as there have been marriages. See if *your* wonderful mother-in-law does any of these things. Would you be surprised if any of her annoying things are on this list? Not!

sits around while everyone else works

complains

smokes

always makes my wife feel bad

won't talk to me

upsets my husband

is judgmental

knows it all

complains about nothing

gives us advice all the time

offers her opinion on everything

is always negative

complains about my wife

complains about Clinton

gives us money, then holds it over our heads

pleads poverty, then buys a new Mercedes

complains about Rush Limbaugh

gives my kids things they are not supposed to have

talks in a foreign language to my husband so I can't understand makes my husband do the dishes

talks too much

complains about violence on TV

lives life like a soap opera

compares my husband to her other children

babies her son

thinks she knows more than I do

only hears what she wants to hear

cheats at cards

doesn't respect my husband

favors her own daughters and hates me

doesn't baby-sit

calls too much

watches soap operas 24 hours a day

is a witch!

thinks she's a jack-of-all-trades

believes she's beautiful

Best answer: "She continually tells me she will outlive every-one."

Have Any of Your Spouse's Friends Come on to You?

	Total
	PERCENT
No	81
Yes	19

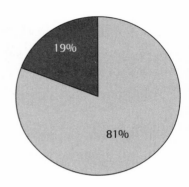

If Yes, Did You Tell?

	Total
	PERCENT
Yes	73
No	27

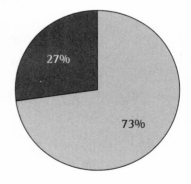

Married less than a year, and 19 percent already have "friends" coming on to their spouses. Now for the surprising stuff (at least to me): More of the "female friends" have come on to the newly-wed husbands than the reverse.

And what happens afterward? Another one of those surprises! Eighty-nine percent of the men tell their wives what happened, while only 33 percent of the women tell their husbands.

Are You Jealous of Your Spouse's Heterosexual Opposite-Sex Friends?

	Total PERCENT	Men PERCENT	Women PERCENT
No	84	69	94
Yes	16	31	6

Men are more jealous of the wife's opposite-sex friends, by a wide margin. Jealous men come in all age, income, and education groups, whether they have been married once, twice, or three times. These men are much more jealous than the women.

An astounding 75 percent of these possessive husbands even put limitations on their wives' friendships with the guys. Limitations include: no visiting when he's not home, no calling, no seeing, letters only (which he gets to read), and absolutely no so-called "friendly" kissing, touching, or feeling.

Are You Attracted to Any of Your Spouse's Friends?

	Total
	PERCENT
■ Yes	14
□ No	86

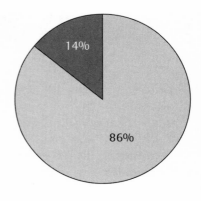

We were afraid of the answers we would get to this question, but fortunately only 14 percent of our newlyweds are attracted to their spouse's friends.

If your spouse is 25 to 34 years old, earns $50,000 to $74,000 a year, and is married for the first time, you might just want to keep your eyes open!

Since You Have Been Married, Have You Propositioned Anyone? Has Anyone Propositioned You?

	Total	Men	Women
	PERCENT	PERCENT	PERCENT
Propositioned Someone			
Yes	3	5	2
No	97	95	98
Propositioned by Someone			
Yes	46	31	55
No	54	69	45

This question is very different from the previous question. This is the real thing, if you know what I mean.

Only a handful of our newlyweds have done the propositioning, while a great many have been the recipients of a proposition. The data show that in both cases they are the young marrieds (18 to 24 years old), married for the first time, and making lots of money. More women have been propositioned than men.

Quite a proposition, don't you think?

Now That You Are Married, Who Makes the Social Arrangements?

	He Says	She Says
	PERCENT	PERCENT
He	15	15
She	27	33
Equal	58	52

The social arrangements are shared equally by the newlyweds more than 53 percent of the time. But it is a woman's thing for the rest of the group, with more than twice as many women taking charge than men (31 percent vs. 15 percent).

In our home, I just follow orders and show up where my wife takes me. My daughters and sons-in-law share the job. What a good idea. But my wife doesn't let me do it yet. She says when I am 70 I can plan one or two days a week.

Do You Prefer to Go Out Alone, Together, or with Another Couple?

	Total PERCENT	Men PERCENT	Women PERCENT
Alone	13	12	13
Together	78	84	75
With Another Couple	9	4	12

Ladies and gentlemen, we have a common decision! Both men and women prefer being alone with their spouse and no one else.

Of the 13 percent who prefer to go out without their spouse, the women are likely to be younger (18 to 24) and the men older (over 40).

One other interesting stat: Of the mere 9 percent who think four's company, most are women!

Now That You Are Married, Is at Least One Night a Week a Boys' or Girls' Night Out?

	Total
	PERCENT
No	82
Yes	18

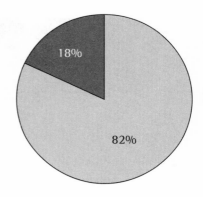

If Yes, Which Night Is It?

	Total
	PERCENT
Boys' night out	26
Girls' night out	19
Both have a night out	55

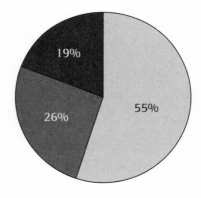

As you can see, most of our newlyweds spend their nights together. However, 18 percent do celebrate a night out alone, and when they do it's generally both partners who have a night on the town.

Would You Allow Your Partner to Go to a Strip Bar?

	Total	Men	Women
	PERCENT	PERCENT	PERCENT
No	45	68	43
Yes	55	32	57

To strip or not to strip, that is the question. While more than half of the newlyweds have no objection to a spouse going to a strip bar, it is interesting that the newlywed women are quicker to allow their husbands to go to a strip bar than the newlywed men are to give their permission.

Those women who do have their husband's blessing are likely to be older (over 40), in a higher income bracket (over $75K a year), and twice married.

If You Had Permission to Go to a Strip Bar, Would You Actually Go?

	Total	Men	Women
	PERCENT	PERCENT	PERCENT
No	75	84	64
Yes	25	16	36

Obviously, our respondents are still very much on their honeymoon. Only 25 percent of the newlyweds would actually go to a strip bar. Believe it or not, it is more likely to be the women (36 percent) than the men (16 percent).

Do You Ever Take Your Wedding Ring Off When You Leave the House?

	Total	Men	Women
	PERCENT	PERCENT	PERCENT
Yes	20	31	14
No	80	69	86

Tsk, tsk! Married only a short time, and already they are taking off their rings when they leave the house. Thirty-one percent of the men are doing so, and 14 percent of the women. (My ring has been on for almost 35 years; it can't come off because my wife had it sealed to my hand.)

The men who are letting their fingers do the walking are likely to be 25 to 39 years old, earning $75,000 or more a year, and have a high school education. Many men who are on their third marriage are also guilty of removing their rings.

Who Does Most of the Driving?

When it comes to driving, it sure is a man's world among newly-weds. Nearly 90 percent of the men do most of the driving.

Is Your Spouse a Better Driver Than You?

Here's a bit of a discrepancy: 98 percent of men and 60 percent of women feel they are the better driver. This sounds like grounds for the first of many tiffs.

If You Get Lost, Will You Stop for Help? Will Your Spouse?

Eighty-five percent of the men and 91 percent of the women claimed they would ask for directions if they were lost. But then how do you explain the next response? Ninety-four percent of the men said their wife will ask for directions if they are lost, while the women informed us that only 23 percent of their spouses will do the same. I must confess that I don't ask for directions until my wife starts yelling at me. Both daughters tell me that luckily their husbands have a great sense of direction. If they do get lost on occasion, neither husband will stop to ask for help.

7
Pleasant Dreams

What Do You Wear to Sleep?

	Total*	Men	Women
	PERCENT	PERCENT	PERCENT
Pajamas	33	24	39
Sweats	5	10	3
Birthday Suit	44	39	49
Underwear	13	21	9
Other	15	7	21

*Adds up to more than 100 percent due to multiple answers

If you catch a female newlywed sleepwalking, you are more than likely to find her in the nude. Forty-nine percent sleep that way, as compared to only 39 percent of the husbands. She is likely to be young (18 to 24 years old), earning a lower income, and married for the first time.

As for the older set, they are the ones who answered OTHER. We can only guess what that means: nightgowns, nightshirts, nightcaps, and who knows what else?

Do You Go to Bed at the Same Time?

	Total	Men	Women
	PERCENT	PERCENT	PERCENT
Yes	73	56	81
No	27	44	19

This appears to be a case of potential hanky-panky. Eighty-one percent of the women say they go to bed at the same time as their spouse, while only 56 percent of the men sing the same tune. My hypothesis is that when the women are asleep, the men catch a second wind and leave.

If you are worried about your man sneaking off, staying up, or doing something else, he is easiest to identify by what he is *not*. He is not 25 to 39 years old, he does not earn $30,000 to $74,000 a year, and it's not his second marriage. Does that help?

Do You and Your Mate Have a Ritual Before You Go to Sleep?

Note: 73 percent go to bed at the same time

	Total*
	PERCENT
☐ Say "I love you"	73
■ Kiss good night	68
▨ Fall asleep holding each other	61
▦ Have sex	20
▨ Call mate at work	5
▤ Other	27

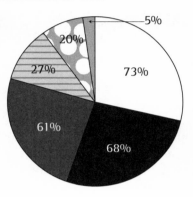

*Adds to more than 100 percent due to multiple answers

What a group of newlyweds! They say "I love you," they kiss, and 20 percent of the time they have sex. With results like these, we sure would like to know what the 27 percent who answered OTHER does, so please ask your friends.

Actually, we did get a few responses in the OTHER category. Some newlyweds try to have sex a second time, even though the spouse is trying to sleep or is already asleep; a few husbands have sex and then go play computer games; a few wives smoke or read or watch TV. Some respondents also told us they pray together after kissing good night and having sex.

How Often Do You Kiss Your Spouse Good Night?

	Total
	PERCENT
Every night	84
A few times a week	13
Once a week	2
Less than once a week	1

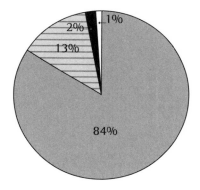

How is it possible that 13 percent of these newlyweds kiss good night only a few times a week, 2 percent do it only once a week, and 1 percent do it less than once a week? C'mon, guys, you're newlyweds; pucker up. My wife and I still do it every night, even after all these years.

8
Fun Statistics

Our newlyweds were married an average of 9.57 months at the time they filled out the questionnaires.

- 68 percent are married for the first time.

- 66 percent had no children at the time, but 13 percent are pregnant. Those who do have children from previous marriages have an average of 2.8 children from his marriage and 2.4 from hers.

- Average age of our newlyweds is 31, with a range of 18 to 89.

- Average household income is $49,569; nearly 80 percent are two-income families. Thirty-five percent earn less than $30,000 a year, and 18 percent earn more than $75,000 a year.

- 66 percent attended or graduated from college.

- 37 percent are urbanites; 14 percent live in rural areas; 49 percent are suburbanites.

- 51 percent live in a single-family home; 39 percent live in an apartment.

- 36 percent of the respondents are male; 64 percent are female.

Complete demographics can be found with the profiles of newlyweds in chapter 11.

9
A Funny Story, a Happy Story, a Sad Story, Anything Goes!

At the end of our questionnaire we asked our newlyweds to tell us something about their engagement and marriage.

We received nearly 2,000 wonderful stories, but due to space limitations we have chosen just a few of them. (Some of the responses were edited, for obvious reasons.)

They will make you laugh, they will make you cry. Enjoy!

◆ ◆ ◆

The most exciting part of our relationship is that we had been 'just friends' for about two years. One night we went to the movies together, and I bought popcorn and a soda for her. As I leaned over to give them to her, our lips brushed and she kissed me. Needless to say, our friendship turned quickly to love and we recently got married. I love her very much.

◆ ◆ ◆

I took her out to a really fancy country club for a romantic candlelight dinner. I had planned the evening by getting us a great table and asking the waiter to put the engagement ring on top of her dessert. However, when we finished our meal she was stuffed and didn't want any dessert. I had to force her to order one. She finally consented, and when she saw the ring she started to cry. It was great. After dinner we walked outside on the golf course, and when we got to the ninth green she asked me to make love to her. I did, and we accidentally fell into the sand bunker. It was truly a night to remember.

◆ ◆ ◆

My fiancé and I spent $740 taking ballroom dancing lessons in the months before our wedding. We couldn't wait to show all of our friends that we could actually dance together. The time came for our first dance. As we walked onto the dance floor, my new husband slipped on a piece of ice and

—would you believe it?—broke his leg. He spent the rest of the wedding reception sitting with his leg elevated on a chair.

◆ ◆ ◆

When my husband and I got married he was just getting a divorce . . . and I mean just. I went with him to get his final papers. We then walked next door and got married within five minutes. I had our baby the next day.

◆ ◆ ◆

I was best friends with my husband's uncle. His uncle and I never dated, but we did have sex together. After one year I moved in with his uncle (just as friends, and for the sex). I fell in love with both the uncle and my husband. I got pregnant, and I think the uncle is the father. I am 15 years older than his uncle and 20 years older than my husband. Now we all live together. My husband still doesn't know about me and his uncle.

◆ ◆ ◆

After we got married we stayed at home for our honeymoon, and I became very sick. At first I thought I had food poisoning. I was vomiting like crazy. My husband ended up taking me to the emergency room. Within a few minutes the vomiting stopped and they told me I did not have food poisoning. It turned out I was four months pregnant. It was the best wedding present anyone could've gotten for us.

◆ ◆ ◆

One night my boss called and asked me to come to his office. My friends thought I was going to get fired, and I was afraid. When I got to his office he told me he loved me. We had sex in his office, and eventually he asked me to marry him. Boy, was I surprised . . . and so were my friends.

◆ ◆ ◆

The bakery that made my wedding cake was held up on my wedding day by a crazed man who wanted to kill himself and the owners of the store. He held them hostage for five hours, until he fell asleep. The baker then escaped and brought my cake to the wedding three hours late. We asked him to stay for the rest of the reception.

◆ ◆ ◆

I don't have a lot to brag about. I've been very disappointed with this marriage. It's my fourth, and I have to stick it out because everyone said it wouldn't last. They were right but I can't let them know. I can't stand this man. He is 78 but looks 95. I am 73. He's short-tempered, self-centered, and generally a pain in the ass. He was a preacher, but he is meaner than a junkyard dog. You see, he is jealous and resentful that I am more educated than he is, so he embarrasses me all the time. I can't tell if he is crazy or what. I just hope I outlive him as I've done with husbands number one and two.

◆ ◆ ◆

I have three children, ages 17, 14, and 10, and my second husband has four children, ages 16, 14, 12, and 10. We got married two months ago, and all the children participated in the wedding party. It was a wonderful day, sort of like the Brady Bunch wedding. Well, I took sick about a week and a half ago and went to see the doctor. I was diagnosed as being pregnant, even though I am 45 years old. When I got home and told my new husband, he fainted. We called all seven kids together and told them. They went absolutely crazy with joy! They kidded us to no end, saying they didn't even know old people did such things. I am going to have this love baby, and the kids can't wait. I have revived my husband, and he is equally thrilled.

◆ ◆ ◆

We got married on horseback. We had twelve horses in the wedding party. The judge came riding up to take his place in front to marry us. As he was riding up the hill, he hit his head on a branch sticking out from a tree and fell off the horse. He started to bleed from just above his eyebrows. He was OK, but dirty and a bit bloody. He took it in stride, regained his composure, and married us while holding a napkin to his bleeding head. After the vows we all trotted off into the sunset to the reception around the barn.

◆ ◆ ◆

We had a very young rabbi perform our wedding ceremony—this was only the second wedding he had ever performed. During the ceremony, he passed me a glass of red wine to taste as part of the blessings. As he passed it to me, it slipped out of his hand and spilled down the front of my beautiful white wedding gown. I believe his face was as red as my dress! I made quite a fashion statement with six white cloth napkins stapled to the front of my dress.

◆ ◆ ◆

My fiancée was eight months pregnant, and we were on our way to the wedding when she went into hard labor. We turned around and went to the hospital. I telephoned the church and told all the guests to come to the hospital. We were married in the delivery room after she gave birth to a beautiful baby boy.

◆ ◆ ◆

Talk about being surprised. When I proposed to my wife, I had set it up beautifully. We went to the circus, and I made sure we had seats in row three. Well, the circus started and the clowns came out and started to pick people randomly from the audience. They picked my soon-to-be-wife and dragged her out along with about ten other people, young, old, men, and women. The ten of them rode on various forms of clown transportation around the ring. After a few minutes, with all the participants now hysterically laughing, they came back to get more people and selected me. Now they were parading all of us around and around until they started doing funny things with balloons and signs and making the little children laugh. Then, for one brief moment, everything stopped and a clown came running out with a sign and he went in front of my lady and turned the sign around to her and it said WILL YOU MARRY ME? She took a moment or two to understand what was going on and then burst into tears of joy. She said yes, and the audience went wild. It was all prearranged by me, through a friend who worked for the stadium.

◆ ◆ ◆

I went with a girlfriend to visit her brother in jail. While there I met his cellmate, and it was love at first sight. I visited him often, and after his five-year sentence was over we were finally able to be together and get married. He is everything I ever wanted in a husband: friend, lover, and companion. He said he was guilty of his crime, armed robbery, but he will never do it again.

◆ ◆ ◆

My bachelor party was very wild. The guys took us back to someone's house, where we drank and drank and drank. We watched X-rated movies, and then the guys brought in two strippers. I was blown away when I saw that one of the strippers was my wife's best friend and soon-to-be maid of honor. She and the other girl grabbed me and took me into another room, where they forced me to have sex with them. It was exciting and terrible at the same time. I was afraid she would tell my wife. A few days later we had a rehearsal for the wedding, and the girl showed up and whispered to me that she would never tell my wife what happened, but that I was now her sex slave whenever she wanted. It is terrible. I don't know what to do. I've been married for three months and she shows up at least once a week and forces me to have sex with her. What am I to do?

◆ ◆ ◆

I dated a lot of jerks who were all interested in the same thing in the 16 years following my divorce. About a month before I met my current husband, I was held up at gunpoint, nearly run over by a truck, and had several girlfriends who were dumped by their guys. Needless to say, I was not thrilled with men at this time! When I met my husband on a blind date I was not very trusting, as you can imagine. However, he quickly showed me that there were still good people out there. He also made me believe in fairy tales. From day one he has made me feel very happy. I'm the happiest I've ever been in my entire life.

◆ ◆ ◆

Both of our spouses passed away, so we attended a bereavement group. We met there and were married after three months. We even have a wonderful sex life at ages 81 and 83! Loved your questions.

◆ ◆ ◆

My sister was staying with us shortly after we were married. My husband and I were going at it hot and heavy. My husband put on a condom and then decided to take it off. As he was taking it off, his hand slipped and the condom snapped right into his privates. He screamed, and I laughed so loud that my sister burst into the room to see what was going on and saw us in this very compromising position. My husband's pain turned to embarrassment. He just about died!

◆ ◆ ◆

This last tale comes from a newlywed of five months.

My husband and I had the most unusual and outrageously sad and funny incident happen all at once to us about two months ago. Just married three months, we were very much still on our honeymoon, very much in love, and having lots and lots of great sex. We enjoyed being alone in our town house with a beautiful bedroom upstairs and the living and dining rooms on the lower level.

My husband's brother and three of his college buddies decided to come and stay with us for ten days on spring break. (We live in Florida.) It was fun to have them stay and they were no bother; they slept downstairs on the couch. They were basically really nice guys.

Early one evening the guys said, "We are going out to rent some movies and have dinner," and asked if we wanted to go with them. We declined. As soon as they left we went upstairs to our bedroom and got into a very heavy, wonderful sexy mood.

As we were making love—and I need to tell you that we were both naked and I (female) was on top—there was a quick knock on the bedroom door and his brother said, "Hi! We're back." I immediately said, "Don't come in yet," but he opened the door and it was as if time stood still. There he was, standing absolutely frozen, and I was naked on top of his brother, equally frozen. It seemed like hours but it was probably ten seconds before he closed the door and ran downstairs.

I was devastated, more concerned for him than for me. I broke down crying and asked my husband what to do. "Your baby brother is probably so humiliated he won't ever face me, talk to me, or have anything to do with me. What am I supposed to do? The poor kid will probably be ruined for life."

My husband calmed me down, and we decided that the best plan would be for me to go downstairs, where he probably was laughing with his buddies about what happened, and break the ice by saying something funny, like "Well, I guess you know that your brother is not a virgin anymore." A silly statement, but I hoped it would clear the air.

I waited about half an hour, got dressed, and went downstairs. As I got to the last two steps, I realized it was very quiet. I was preparing my funny speech, when I saw the four guys sitting on our couch, reading newspapers, and they all were naked. I was so shocked I couldn't breathe. The four of them stood up and dropped the newspapers, and appeared in front of me, totally naked. We all began to laugh. My husband rushed downstairs to see what the commotion was, and he nearly fainted.

It turned out that the fears of my brother-in-law and I were the same. We both thought we would never forget what had happened, but we quickly broke the ice and had a tremendous laugh about it, too.

10
What They Didn't Tell Us

While writing this book, I found it quite interesting to look at my statistics and find out what things the respondents *didn't* tell us. I did this by looking at the percentages of people who for one reason or another chose not to answer a particular question. Why do you think our newlyweds took the fifth on the following? Remember, as you read these stats, that none of the newlyweds gave us their names, so there was no reason not to answer.

- 26 percent did not answer whether they kissed and/or slept together on their first date.
- 1 percent could not remember the first time they slept together.
- 4 percent could not remember how long they dated before they were engaged.
- 10 percent wouldn't tell us how often they made love on their honeymoon.
- 8 percent wouldn't tell us if they had had sex before marriage.
- 9 percent clammed up as to who controlled the remote for the TV.
- 8 percent wouldn't divulge who took care of the money.
- 3 percent couldn't remember if they had asked their partner to change his/her lovemaking techniques.
- 4 percent couldn't remember how often they had sex before marriage.
- 11 percent wouldn't tell us how often they had sex in the last month.

11
Profiles of the Respondents

Who are our newlywed respondents? They come from all 50 states and all walks of life. Thirty-six percent are male and 64 percent female.

Age

Our average newlywed is 31 years old.

- 28 percent are 18 to 24.
- 48 percent are 25 to 34.
- 15 percent are 35 to 49.
- 9 percent are 50 or older. In this group, the youngest is 50 and the oldest is 89!

Income

Our newlyweds are quite well heeled compared to the general population. They have an average combined yearly income of $49,569. The major reason for the high income is that both partners work in more than 80 percent of our households.

- 35 percent have a yearly income under $30,000.
- 26 percent have a yearly income between $30,000 and $49,999.
- 21 percent have a yearly income between $50,000 and $74,999.
- 18 percent have a yearly income of $75,000 or more.

Education

- 34 percent have a high school education.
- 66 percent have attended or graduated from college.

Living Areas

3,876 newlyweds in all 50 states responded.

- 37 percent are urbanites.
- 14 percent live in rural America.
- 49 percent are suburbanites.
- 51 percent live in a private home.
- 10 percent live in a multifamily home.
- 39 percent live in an apartment.

Length of Time Married

The average newlyweds in our survey have been married for 9.57 months.

- 12 percent have been married from 0 to 3 months.
- 37 percent have been married from 4 to 6 months.
- 27 percent have been married from 7 to 9 months.
- 24 percent have been married 10 months or more.

Number of Times Married

- 68 percent of our newlyweds are married for the first time.
- 25 percent of our newlyweds have been married twice.
- 5 percent of our newlyweds have been married three times.
- 2 percent of our newlyweds have been married four or more times.

Sidelights: The newlyweds in our survey who were married *before* this marriage were married for an average of 8.1 years in their first marriage. The shortest marriage lasted three days and the longest lasted 40 years.

The second marriages lasted for an average of 8.2 years. The shortest lasted one month, and the longest lasted 26 years.

The third marriages lasted for an average of 4.6 years, from one month to 13 years.

Children

Newlyweds who have been previously married have an average of 2.8 children from his previous marriage and 2.4 children from her previous marriage.

- 66 percent of our newlyweds have no children yet.
- 34 percent of our newlyweds have children, most from previous marriages. Of these newlyweds, 2 percent already have a child from their latest partner.
- 13 percent of our newlyweds are now pregnant.

Good luck to all our newlyweds!

About the Authors

Barry Sinrod's humor comes from his roots—the Coney Island section of Brooklyn, New York. In 1992, at age 49, Barry retired to Boca Raton, Florida, with his wife Shelly after a very successful career in marketing research. Barry and Shelly have three children and five grandchildren.

As a student of fun and statistics, Barry lists his biographical achievements as follows:

Several *great* days in his life:

1. Listening to play-by-play of the Florida Marlins' victory in Game Seven of the 1997 World Series via his son, Blake, on the telephone at 4:45 A.M. Barry was in Nice, France, at the time and the phone bill was $115.

2. Seeing Barbra Streisand in concert in 1967 in Central Park, and again twenty-nine years later at Madison Square Garden.

3. Spending a weekend with Steven Spielberg and watching all his movies in upstate New York. At the same time, Barry had a beard and looked a very, very little bit like Steven and someone actually came over to him and gave him a script to look at.

4. A lifelong New York Giants fan and season-ticket holder for thirty-five years (even though he now lives full-time in Florida), he attended both Super Bowls XXI and XXV, which the Giants won.

5. Experiencing the joy on his daughter's face when after having two boys, she gave birth to a girl.

6. Not many fans have had the good fortune of seeing their hometown sports team win a championship in person, but Barry has more than once. He was there when the Brooklyn Dodgers won the World Series, and again when the New York Mets won it. He also saw the New York Islanders win several Stanley Cup Championships. Oh, the joys of being born in Brooklyn!

Marlo Grey is a first-time author. She enjoyed coauthoring this book with her father and hopes to continue writing, perhaps even venturing into children's books in the future. Marlo is also a wife and a mother of two. Raising two boys under two years of age keeps her extremely busy and extremely happy.